STEPHEN L. THOMAS

Printed in the United States of America

First Printing, 2025

978-1-961278-02-8

Stephen L. Thomas | Established 2022 | USA

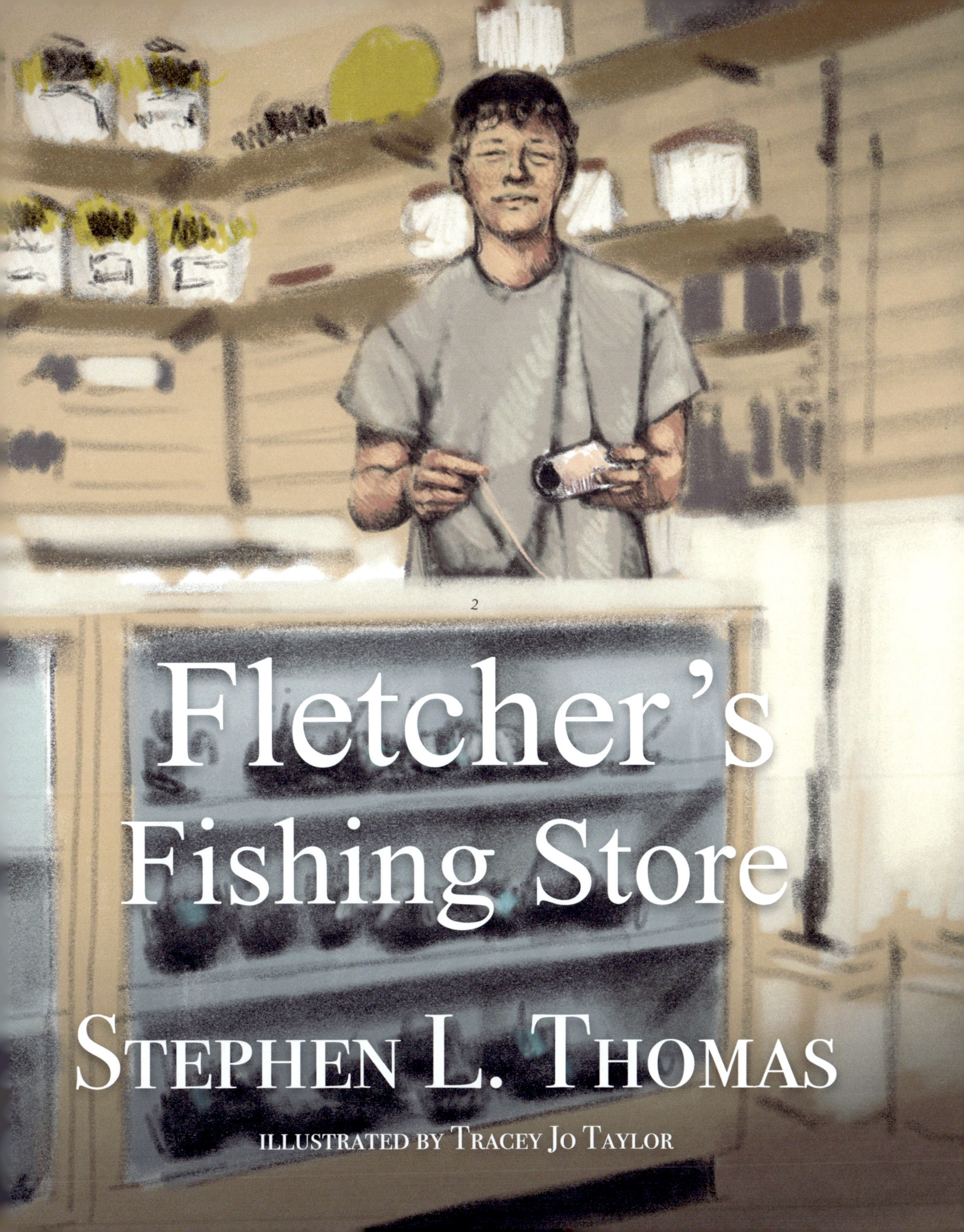

2

Fletcher's Fishing Store

Stephen L. Thomas

illustrated by Tracey Jo Taylor

It was a warm and sunny morning, Jacob and Bobby woke up excited, remembering that today was the day Dad promised to take them fishing. As they headed out the door with their fishing rods in hand, mom tucked some packed lunches into a backpack and handed it to them. "You three have a great time and catch some big fish!"

"Big ones only!" Bobby shouted. Jacob and Dad smiled and nodded in agreement.

They all threw their fishing rods into the back of Dad's red pickup truck and drove down the road with the windows down––the music turned up, and off they went to Cato Lake!

Before arriving at the lake, Dad pulled into the gravel parking lot at Fletcher's. Everything looked the same as last year: the dark green paint on the front door, the tin sign that said, 'Gone Fishin', and the wilting sunflower outside the window. But, this time, something else was there too. On the bench next to the door, they noticed a boy, about the same age as Jacob and Bobby, sitting with his head down, looking really sad.

shing Store
GONE
FISHIN'

As they all got out of the truck, Jacob asked, "Dad, what was wrong with the boy?" "I'm not sure, but let's ask and see if we can help." So, they all walked over to the bench where the boy was sitting. "Hi there," greeted Dad and asked the boy's name. However, the boy didn't look up. "Son, you can tell us what's wrong. I'm sure we can try to help," Dad suggested. With his head down, the boy responded, "I'm Okay." Jacob and Bobby looked at Dad, expecting that he would know what to do, but Dad could see that the boy wouldn't say anything more. Gently patting the boy on the shoulder, Dad said, "We'll see you on the way out."

When they walked into the shop, Fletcher, who had been untangling a s pool of fishing line, looked up from behind the counter and smiled. "Well, look who it is!" He exclaimed as he made his way over to greet them. After shaking each of their hands, he said, "Today's a great day for fishing, boys! I heard they're biting on minnows. You need some?" Bobby responded, "Yes sir! That's why we came!"

"Great! Right this way," replied Fletcher as he led them over to the bait section.

After they had picked out the right minnows, they walked back to the counter. Dad gave each of the boys an extra ten-dollar bill. "You boys can use this to buy something now, or you can save it for later," Dad said.

"Thank you, Dad!" Bobby knew right away what he wanted to do with his ten dollars. He ran to the back shelf and grabbed a blue hat that had a "Fletcher's" logo on it with a big, silver fish. Fletcher looked at Jacob and said, "Young man, what do you want to do with your ten dollars?" Jacob thought for a minute and said, "I think I'd like to buy two cold root beers and two bags of peanuts." So, Fletcher grabbed two cold root beers from the fridge. He then rang up the minnows, the hat, drinks, and peanuts separately and handed each boy back their change, which they both tucked into their jean pockets. Bobby received fifty cents back, and Jacob received five dollars and fifty cents.

After thanking Fletcher, they headed out the door and back into the hot summer sun. Outside, they looked around to see if the boy was still there, but he was nowhere in sight. "Dad, where do you think he went?" Jacob asked. "I'm not sure," Dad responded. So, they all got back in the truck.

They headed towards the lake down the bumpy dirt road next to Fletcher's. Surely enough, they saw the boy walking on the side of the road with his head down. "There's the boy," Jacob yelled. Dad drove up and pulled over near the boy. Jacob jumped out with a root beer in one hand and peanuts and money in the other. He walked up to the boy and said, "Hey! You don't have to talk to me if you don't want to, but I thought you may be thirsty and need help." Jacob said as he handed the boy the root beer, peanuts, and money. Slowly, the boy looked up and said, "Thank you." Jacob could see the tear stains around his eyes. As Jacob turned to walk back to the truck, the boy called over to him. "What's your name?" Jacob stopped and turned around. "My name's Jacob," he smiled. "What's yours?" "Andrew." "It's good to meet you, Andrew. I thought you might want a root beer and some peanuts; they're my favorites!" "Mine too!" Andrew laughed. As Dad drove away, Jacob and Bobby rolled down their window and yelled, "Have a great day, Andrew!" "Thanks, Jacob! I hope to see you again!" Andrew yelled back.

Finally, they arrived at their secret fishing spot on Lake Cato. There, they each took turns putting minnows on their lines and casting them into the water.

As they sat on the bank of the lake, patiently waiting for the fish to bite, Dad said, "Jacob, I'm very proud of what you did back there for Andrew. It appeared he was hurting and needed to be encouraged. You saw a need and went out of your way to help him." Bobby was sitting on the other side of Dad listening, and chimed in, "But Dad, how do we know if what Jacob gave Andrew was what he needed?"

"We don't, but sometimes in life you still need to act, even when you don't know all the answers. Especially, when you see someone in need. All acts of kindness are a blessing to a person, and even if Andrew didn't need something to drink, eat, or money, he might know someone else who does."

"Wow!" Bobby responded, "I never thought about it like that." Bobby turned to Jacob and said, "I'm glad you gave Andrew your money. I want to give you my hat!" With a surprised look, Jacob said, "But I thought you loved your new hat?" "I do! But you blessed Andrew, and seeing you do that made me wish I had done it too. So, I want to bless you!" said Bobby. The brothers high-fived each other, and then they all spent the rest of the afternoon telling jokes, eating their delicious, packed lunches, and catching a lot of big fish!

"It's funny, Dad," Jacob said from the backseat. "It made me even happier when I gave the money to Andrew than when you gave me the money in the store." Bobby added, "I felt better, too, when I gave you the hat than when I bought it for myself in the first place." Seeing the boys laugh through the rear-view mirror, their Dad smiled.

"You both learned two valuable things about money today. First, it's better to give than to receive, and second, giving to others not only blesses them but also gives them the power to bless others. I'm proud of you both!"

As Jacob and Bobby lay in bed that night, Bobby said to Jacob, "I'm proud to have you as my brother! I have an idea: Why don't we go tomorrow after school and buy Ms. Little some groceries with what I earned? Afterward, we can mow a couple of yards and earn extra money so that we can do Ms. Little's yard for free!" Jacob smiled, "Bobby, you're the best brother in the whole world!"

Notes From the Author:

When we earn or are given money, it's fun to think about ways to spend it. As we grow older, if we learn to be wise with money by keeping the four principles of "save a little, spend a little, give a little, and you'll always have a little," what you will find over time is that not only will you have more than you ever wished for or needed, but, like Bobby giving Jacob his hat and Jacob blessing Andrew, blessing others with your overflow will become a regular part of your life.

All too often, when we earn more money, our spending increases as well—which can limit our savings, investments, and giving. One of the best things about money is when we learn to spend and invest wisely. We will always have money to help those like Andrew. It's funny how we seldom consider that after helping someone, they, in turn, can help others when they have the resources to do so. It's not just about helping one person; the ripple effects can be felt by many. You see, Jacob's act of kindness to bless Andrew may have meant a lot to him and perhaps even his family. He may have given Andrew a lasting memory of hope and possibly a smile on his mother's face, who may have been praying for her son to be encouraged or to meet a new friend. Imagine the next time you were at a restaurant and bought dinner for a single mom and her child or had an opportunity to buy someone a cup of coffee waiting in line behind you—groceries for an older lady who may be a widow or even wash a neighbor's car. It's important to remember that having money gives you power, but there are two forms of power: the power to consume, which only blesses one person (you), and the power to bless others!

The power to bless only yourself disappears at the time of purchase and is easily forgotten. At the same time, the power to bless others lasts forever. So, like Jacob, who blessed Andrew, he was not only given the gift of a new friend, but he also blessed Bobby, who later wanted to bless him in return.

Imagine how incredible the world would be if we all gave from what we have, like Bobby and Jacob. I hope you enjoy this story about Fletcher's Fishing Store as much as I have enjoyed writing it.

Stephen L. Thomas

★ ★ ★ HELPFUL IDEAS ★ ★ ★

FOR PARENTS TO HELP CHILDREN PAY IT FORWARD!

No matter your age, there are always ways you can be managing your money well and helping those in need. Here are some ideas!

✓	Ways To Pay It Forward
	Pay for someone in line behind you at checkout
	Give out personalized compliment cards
	Write letters and mail them to those who may feel lonely
	Return someone else's shopping cart to the bay
	Mow a neighbors lawn
	Give clothing and toys to those in need
	Give a Homeless person some food/essentials bag
	Give up your seat on the bus
	Let someone go ahead of you in checkout
	Bake home goods for local fire/police departments
	Give a box of candy and a handwritten card to your Postal worker
	Create a "Pay it Forward" Jar for coins to use when its full on paying it forward.

Always Remember:

ALL HARD WORK LEADS TO PROSPERITY AND WHEN YOU BLESS OTHERS, GOD BLESSES YOU!

Made in the USA
Las Vegas, NV
08 November 2026

57691393R00021